KING DAVIDS TRIUMPH

BELIEF IN CHANGE ALL THAT IS REQUIRED FOR GREATNESS.

TABLE OF CONTENT   PAGE NO

DEDICATION   3

ACKNOWLEDGMENT   4

INTRODUCTION   5

MY TRIUMPH   6

WHY DO I NEED CHANGE   9

EFFECT OF CHANGE   11

WAYS TO STAND FIRM DURING CHANGE   15

WHAT IS IN JOY   20

DEDICATION

To every soul, going through pain; during and after the pandemic caused by Covid-19 outbreak.

Acknowledgment

To our God, ABBA father who has never failed the Christian associations all over the world, building and preserving our faith as we contend daily for the price set before us.

There comes a point in everyone's life, when the question of their true existence becomes a thing of utmost concern. For most people, curiosity, passion even pain pops up the question. We tend to live with so much distractions either from work, taking care of family, or distracted by friends and lifestyle; that we don't really know that every man has a solemn reason to why they are called into these world, given to us by a loving God. Never forget there is a spiritual warfare going on in the world; God is choosing his armies by the day, same as satan. Everyone has projected a pattern through which the achieve this goal, satan will stop at nothing trying to use pain to distract the world, that is why this article is written to encourage everyone going through any form of pain. There is still HOPE. Fashion is great, art is wonderful, and most of these tools have been a pointer of distraction to turn the face of man from the real truth of why he was created. Ever since the fall of man in the garden of Eden, man hasn't gained full control of his dominion towards the earth, because Satan has been using age advantage to deceive man. Look at the world we live in, there is so much pain, crisis everywhere, agony in the heart of men. This pain has made man to seek happiness and joy in the wrong things; making man stay deceived every day of his life while satan enjoys man's supposed dominion. Many people in the world assume that God is the cause of their predicament, Luke 11:13 says **"If ye then, being evil, know how to give good gifts unto your children: how much more shall your heavenly Father give the Holy Spirit to them that ask him?"** God can never think evil or wickedness towards his children.

Let your faith connect you......

MY TRIUMPH

This article is for strengthening of the faith of everyone who might have faced one challenge or the other all through and after the pandemic; those whose faith went cold on God. Let this article inspire you to build back your faith. The purpose of this book is to give hope to everyone in Diaspora. Many people lost their loved ones, family members, colleagues; some lost their jobs, companies, firms. We all in one way or the other lost something valuable, something we hold dearest. While you read this book, I hope it gives your heart the light it needs to glow again; because HOPE is all that we need. At this point, so many of us are still isolated in one way or the other; dealing with pain, caused by this Pandemic. Man is an emotional being; we all deal with pain and change differently. During this pandemic, we saw on the internet people who committed suicide; either for the loss of loved ones, loss of company, firms, and the truth still remains that; most firms are kept alive on the oxygen of loan and mortgages. Everyone can't handle pain and change same way; some of the people who died are breadwinners of their families, now the families are left without hope of any sort. Some are the only hope their families are banking and investing on. Whatever be the situation, I want to encourage someone reading this book; suicide isn't an option at all. All we need is Hope; hope always begets a good walk with change; basically with a change of mindset. While dealing with any kind of pain, change is much more vital than any other thing one could consider. Victor Marie Hugo a French poet, novelist, and dramatist once said "progress is man's mode of existence"; without change, there isn't progress. It is normal for everyone to have the fear of change, because change comes with pain. It reminds us of our failure, our past, everything we didn't have the power to make right. The truth still remains, without pain, there isn't any growth. At this time everyone is dealing with heartbreak caused by the pandemic, the fear of starting fresh, outgrowing the pain and all sorts of things fear triggers. But I would like to remind you that; even the awesome creator of the universe, gave man the grace of improving through change at every point in time. Of all creatures, man is the only being that has this grace; so why complain? Why stay in fear? When the creator let us know through his word in Jeremiah 29:11 ; **For I know the thoughts that I think toward you, saith the LORD, thoughts of peace, and not of evil, to give you an expected end"**. God blessed man with memory for stimulus sequences, which distinguishes us from other creatures; and with that alone, man can adapt any change that comes his path. Bee doesn't improve the process after making its first sweet honey; neither does the bird, after singing its first melody, or even wolves improving their howling. Change is like an ingredient, to help man improve himself; it is only fear that limits most people who get laid back. There is a tiny line between, the pain we feel and stepping into a new life, that tiny line is accepting to make a change. When we fail to accept change, we become dangerously structured dams, blocking the inflow of progress which in no time would definitely keep affecting us physically, and spiritually. When we get damaged spiritually, there is every tendency of inflicting same pain to others, thereby distributing the pain. In 1st Samuel 18 vs 6-11, after David killed Goliath; King Saul become bitter and jealous, to the point of attempting to pin David to the wall with his spear; but he didn't succeed in that quest. Just because he couldn't handle the pain jealousy secreted in his heart. One thing we must not forget, there is a greater good in every situation we find ourselves in; and when we realize that; every stumbling block, be it heartbreak, pain of the past, whatsoever that burdens our heart becomes a stepping stone. All that is needed is to accept the situation and cling to hope for the greater good, the future would definitely birth. While going through the journey of life, like every precious jewel; our lives get subjected to fire. It could be fire of rejection, fire of lost, fire of shattered dreams, fire of forced solitude; we get tested at every point in our lives; what truly matters is the mind eyes we set on hope; that alone would definitely make us step out of the fire with both stronger mind and body. Receiving grace, we could carry a bucket of water out of it, to help others who can't deal with their own fire. Your persistence to holding strong and setting your eyes on hope; will always inspire someone else going through same huddle in life. Like the potter's relationship with fire while harnessing the precious jewel; mastery is all that is required of us. When you accept change, and get your body and soul ready for a greater good; every pain, bitterness, forced solitude, and weakness becomes a stepping stone to attain a new height. While we're suffering through the disheartening pain of loss, heartbreak, shattered hope, forced solitude, failure, we're often not thinking about making a change, we're solely focused on surviving. When we go through all of this pain, it makes us question everything, right down to the very course and purpose of our existence. Pain, as much as it hurts, is also a necessary part of life. It's the pathway to our goals, to us giving life a new shot through accepting change.

WHY DO I NEED CHANGE?

One can't cling to the past and remain stuck in it at all times, it will definitely block the inflow of a better us thereby eluding us our greater future. As you're going through the torrent of pain right now, know this, Pain with constructive plan towards change will make you better. It will definitely improve your life. The most successful and famous people in the world have endured the most pain in life. They've failed repeatedly, they have faced rejection, they have lost firms, ideas gone and buried, and they have gone through fire, now they keep the fire blazing. They've gotten back up. They didn't throw in that proverbial towel; they didn't call it quits or head for the ropes for suicide. They got up and kept going; that's just what it takes to create a new you through constructive change. Constructive change, demands us to have iron will regardless of how many times we fail in life;

every failure, pain; well managed, results to greater good. Ella Wheeler Wilcox, an American author and poet ones wrote

Upon the wreckage of thy yesterday
Design the structure of tomorrow. Lay
Strong corner stones of purpose, and prepare
Great blocks of wisdom, cut from past despair.
Shape mighty pillars of resolve, to set
Deep in the tear-wet mortar of regret.
Work on with patience. Though thy toil be slow,
Yet day by day the edifice shall grow.
Believe in God--in thine own self believe.
All that thou hast desired thou shalt achieve.

Ella Wheeler Wilcox also wrote this poem of solitude, which gives us a better understanding of pain in solitude; be it forced or self indulged solitude. Which is a quick reminder that, at all times; we owe it to our self, to stay strong regardless of what put us down. There is a greater good in every change, keep your three eyes (The two eyes with which you see and your mind eye) stuck on hope.

Laugh, and the world laughs with you;
Weep, and you weep alone;
For the sad old earth must borrow its mirth,
But has trouble enough of its own.

Sing, and the hills will answer;

Sigh, it is lost on the air;

The echoes bound to a joyful sound,

But shrink from voicing care.

Rejoice, and men will seek you;

Grieve, and they turn and go;

They want full measure of all your pleasure,

But they do not need your woe.

Be glad, and your friends are many;

Be sad, and you lose them all,—

There are none to decline your nectared wine,

But alone you must drink life's gall.

Feast, and your halls are crowded;

Fast, and the world goes by.

Succeed and give, and it helps you live,

But no man can help you die.

There is room in the halls of pleasure

For a large and lordly train,

But one by one we must all file on

Through the narrow aisles of pain.

Effect of Change

In whatever situation life put us through, in whatever fire life tends to test our integrity, our patience, our temperament, our loyalty, we must not forget; there is a greater Being who watches over the affairs of man. Daniel 2:21 **"He changes the times and seasons; He removes kings and establishes them. He gives wisdom to the wise and knowledge to the discerning"**.

Human being, irrespective of the blessing of memory for stimulus sequences, our awesome creator of the universe blessed us with; tend to forget easily our root, letting pain and challenges win our dear soul and body. The truth is, we can't always handle everything by our power, when we descend that He may ascend in us; every season of pain becomes a stepping stone for a greater good. Let me quickly introduce you to some great minds like us, who also went through fire and the obvious greater good they came out of it with, even carrying buckets of water for those still burned by the fire.

> ➢ **Colonel Harland Sanders**

At the ripe young age of 5-years old, his father died, leaving only his mother to fend for and support three children, at the age of 12-years old, his mother remarried, subjecting the children to an arduous environment that ultimately forced Harland to leave home the following year. Harland worked odd jobs for years, lost his firms but with just a $105 social security check to his name, at the age of 65-years old, he set out to sell his franchised-chicken model to restaurants across the country. He was famously rejected by 1,009 restaurants before one agreed to his idea. Colonel Harland Sanders, is the founder of Kentucky Fried Chicken (KFC), which is famous only for his chicken recipe; now being enjoyed all over the world. Currently, having an approximate 24,000 employees; all over the world. This is truly a man with iron will, whose dogged perseverance set him out of the fire bearing buckets of water for those burning in the fire of unemployment.

➢ Oprah Winfrey

Born to a single teenage mother; Winfrey grew up in a sheer state of utter poverty for most of her childhood life, living with her grandmother during those years. When she was 6-years old, she moved in with her mother in Wisconsin, during those early years, Winfrey says she was sexually molested by her cousin, her uncle and a family friend. At the age of 13-years old, she ran away from home. At 14-years old, she was pregnant and gave birth prematurely to a baby that died shortly after birth. After several failures and pain of losses; today Oprah Winfrey Show has became the highest-ranked talk-show in Chicago. Today, she is a multi-billionaire and has had a major impact on a large part of the world. This is woman who suffered pain from childhood, but didn't let that put her to the rope of suicide. Her company is estimated to have about 787 employees.

➢ Steve Jobs

In his earliest days, Jobs felt unwanted. He was put up for adoption by his mother and was raised by a blue-collar couple in Palo Alto, California. He dropped out of college and started taking the courses that were most interesting to him rather than trying to complete his degree. Afterwards, Jobs co-founded Apple Computers with his friend, Steve Wozniak; the company still faced lots of challenges Jobs resigned from Apple and quit, taking 5 employees with him to start his new business venture, NeXT. That disheartening period helped to embolden Jobs. While Apple was fledgling and would eventually be on the verge of bankruptcy, NeXT thrived. Ultimately, NeXT was acquired by Apple in 1997 bringing him back into the stream of a now giant company. As at 2019 apple has an estimate of 137,000 employees. One of the greatest pain one can go through in life, is the pain of rejection especially from family; Jobs didn't allow that put him down. He persevered regardless of his then situation.

➢ King David

This article is more about bringing to light, King David's life of dogged perseverance and how he dealt with pain and seasons of change to become a man after God's heart. After he was anointed King, one might think that's the end of crises for young David; but that was when his test on fire erupted. David suffered rejection, loss, betrayal, and it was mostly in the hands of those he loved. From King Saul, whom he was loyal to, risking his life to fight and killing Goliath; instead of getting warm hugs and appreciation, King Saul became so jealous to the point of being desperate to take young David's life. Amnon one of King David's son raped his half sister Tamar, for that reason Absalom plotted and killed his brother Amnon. Imagine the pain King David was living with at that point in his life, but Seven times a day; he worshipped God. He never sorted out for the ropes, to make the journey an easy one for him. Absalom plotted against King David, to take his life and claim his throne; which made him flee Jerusalem. Absalom publicly had intercourse with his father's concubines just to take his kingdom from him while he was still alive. All I can see in King David is a man of great iron will; who knew the secret to connecting to our awesome God regardless of what season his life is experiencing.

NOTE: Remember, those who survive change in seasons; are those who never gave up their belief, that their life had a meaning despite everything going on around them, because they understand that, the phase of that current season of pain would definitely end. Sense of purpose, is what gives our lives a meaning, no matter the current situation of things, learning how to constructively make a change out of the situation is the key to achieving a greater goal.

Ways to stand firm during change in seasons

- **CONVICTION OF A GREATER BEING**

That deep emotional conviction of the presence of a superior reasoning power, which is revealed in the incomprehensible universe, forms my idea of God. "Albert Einstein"

The universe is crystal evidence, that everything concerning life is uncertain. There are changing times and moments, as long as we exist and breathe; change is constant. Nature, being very accommodating to both human and everything therein; at some point very cruel, to the point of taking virtually everything we love and care about. Regardless, we must recognize a greater being; who in all of our pain and agony; has his hands always stretched out to welcome us in his bosom of peace with love. Human being, sometimes think of themselves as strong enough to do it all, not recognizing the uncertainties of life; that's why we get to break down at the slightest point of negative change in our lives. When we take a good look at everything around us, from the stretching of heaven, to the boundaries of the oceans, the soil sitting strongly on top of water to produce food and medication for both man and all inhabitants of this universe; to the consciousness of man's ability to produce and reproduce, all of these, and many more; is a sign to let us know there is greater power than life itself, invisibly existing amongst us. The recognition of the carrier of that power; is the conviction we all need; to joyfully live in these world in peace and harmony, regardless of the inevitable uncertainties that might sprout up at any given time. This strong conviction will walk us through phase of life's negative change, when it happens without the thoughts of ending a life just for a phase that won't stay forever. Man is either made or unmade by himself, in the arsenal of his own thoughts, he builds the tools required to give him true joy and happiness. True happiness is attained when our lives is cling to a greater being, walking us through life's pain; holding our hands in assurance of his love. Philippians 4:6-7 **"Do not be anxious about anything, but in every situation, by prayer and petition, with thanksgiving, present your requests to God"**. And the peace of God, which transcends all understanding, will guard your hearts and your minds in Christ Jesus." When we are faced with life's challenges, we get too anxious; that we tend to forget there is a greater being who oversees the affairs of man. Wondered why beautiful, sweet looking roses have thorns around them? The thorns are not there to harm them, rather; thorns are there to serve as protective adaptation from predators. What could ever be as beautiful and sweet as human? Vessel God made in his own image, gave charge over all things created, also bestowed man the power of creation and recreation. The hardship, the pain, the forced solitude man go through, isn't always for a bad objective; sometimes, this pains are actually there for us to find ourselves; after which, gain the power to recreate our mind. Pain is always there to give us a new mind, Perhaps, we have been thinking low of ourselves; pain is there to serve as a boost towards positive thinking. For whatsoever a man thinketh, so he is. God still remains in the business of recreating man, through changing circumstances; when we open our heart and accept these changes, a new us is birth. We also get to enjoy the inherent good in us, for every soul; there is an inherent good that exist within, which is greater than the troubling surface we pay more attention to. Walking with the strong conviction of God; makes the good within keep us glowing, even in times of challenges. Difficulties come in diverse forms, some challenges aren't drastic tragedy, but the busy chaos of managing life; there is no such thing as pointless pain in the life of a child of God. Hebrews 12: 10 **"For they disciplined us for a little while as seemed good to them, but he does so for our benefit, that we may share his holiness"** God enables us to share in His holiness through the discipline of enduring hardship; discipline is a sign of God's love. Trials make it clear to the world that we are not in control. Everyone can see that we don't have the ability or strength to overcome all problems. Therefore, when God works, he gets all the glory; we get to see his hand in all things he does. Romans 5:3-5 **"We rejoice in our sufferings, knowing that suffering produces endurance, and endurance produces character, and character produces hope, and hope does not put us to shame, because God's love has been poured into our hearts through the Holy Spirit who has been given to us"** Apostle Paul wrote in Corinthians, Five different times the Jewish leaders gave me thirty-nine lashes, three times I was beaten with rods. Once I was stoned. Three times I was shipwrecked. Once I spent a whole night and a day adrift at sea. I have traveled on many long journeys. I have faced danger from rivers and from robbers. I have faced danger from my own people, the Jews, as well as from the Gentiles. I have faced danger in the cities, in the deserts, and on the seas. And I have faced danger from men who claim to be believers but are not. But in all things I give thanks to God, the father of our lord Jesus. Apostle Paul was convinced about a greater power, stronger than he is; who is always there to comfort him. Romans 8:36-39 says "36 **As it is written, For thy sake we are killed all the day long; we are accounted as sheep for the slaughter. 37 Nay, in all these things we are more than conquerors through him that loved us. 38 For I am persuaded, that neither death, nor life, nor angels, nor principalities, nor powers, nor things present, nor things to come, 39 Nor height, nor depth, nor any other creature, shall be able to separate us from the love of God, which is in Christ Jesus our Lord"**. With everything King David went through, seven times a day he went to the temple to worship and give thanks to God. King David even in the midst of all the burning fire around him, never threw away his conviction of the greater being who consistently provides, protects, and keep increasing him. Every time we go through fire, bear in mind; this is your test of love of God. Nothing will ever separate us from the love of God, let the situation teach you spiritual building of your love for God. Whatever you lost, believe that God is ever ready and willing to restore all that. Stay joyful and rejoice! Rejoice evermore!

- **Remain ever joyful**.

Staying joyful in times of trials may seem impossible, personally; I went through same change during pandemic. In Africa, people get to do all sorts of diabolical practice all for the sake of making wealth without stress. I lived with a best friend of 8 years in the eastern region of Nigeria; I cherished our friendship so much, I gave all my trust to the friendship believing that we are working together towards achieving a given goal of success. Little did I know, my supposed best friend had sold his soul to the devil, and needed to use my star as a tool to shine on earth; funny as it may sound, he is a priest in a Jewish congregation. Never knew he harvest stars, he poisoned my body system through meals we ate at home using all sorts of charms to weaken me spiritually. One fateful day, after he had stolen my toothbrush to use as a contact for the witchcraft practice, he kept the charm for me in a bedside drawer using money to conjure the charm. When I saw this, it donned on me why he stole my toothbrush, I was heartbroken beyond measure. I lost joy for years, healing seemed impossible at that time. All I did was get into prayer, some days I couldn't pray; all I did was cry. Truth be told, it took a year plus couple of months to begin my healing. God brought joy into my life, because I asked for it; Matthew 7:7 says "**Ask, and it shall be given you; seek, and ye shall find; knock, and it shall be opened unto you**" I held onto this word in prayer, and joy was supplied onto me. When you don't ask, how then can you receive? I was busy crying, which could seem normal, but didn't pay attention that I was dealing with a man; devil can use at anytime to do his dirty works, my attention is meant to remain on God, who will do everything possible to restore my joy; whom is ever trustworthy. I know some of us make this mistake due to ignorance, we have lost friends, family members and loved ones who promised to be there for us but turned serpent to bite us. 1 peter 4:13 says "**But rejoice, inasmuch as ye are partakers of Christ's sufferings; that, when his glory shall be revealed, ye may be glad also with exceeding**

joy. Sometimes, life hits us hard just to break our heart, bearing in mind the pain Christ endured on the cross for our sake; gives my heart a pointer to endure whatever I pass through. We live in a world full of wickedness, who is the source of all these wickedness? Luke 13:16 makes it clear to us **"And ought not this woman, being a daughter of Abraham, whom Satan hath bound, lo, these eighteen years, be loosed from this bond on the sabbath day?** Satan held someone bound that she was bent for 18 years, till Christ healed her; imagine the pain the woman had endured all those years of walking bent; this is to let you understand who the source of wickedness is. For this reason, we have to remain joyful at all times; because all that he desires is that every believer remains bitter and sad. Thank God for Christ who willingly gave us his Blood on the cross of Calvary to save us from the bondage of Satan and his cohorts. 1 Thessalonians 5:16 encourages us to Rejoice evermore. It is for a purpose of securing our heart of gratitude to God; despising every appearances of evil. Joy is one of the tools in the kingdom to keep satan stranded.

What is in Joy?

1. Joy is the undeniable source of strength

When we stay joyful, we are full of strength, for sadness dries the bone making us weak, when the bone which is man's physical support system; man would definitely be weak. Nehemiah 8:10 says **"Then he said unto them, Go your way, eat the fat, and drink the sweet, and send portions unto them for whom nothing is prepared: for this day is holy unto our**

Lord: neither be ye sorry; for the joy of the LORD is your strength.** When we stay joyful we are giving our body every portion of supplement to stay healthy. Proverbs 17:22 says "**A merry heart doeth good like a medicine: but a broken spirit drieth the bones.** Joy is compared to medicine which does good to the body, imagine taking this medicine every day of your life; how about an overdose of this medicine. Joy can never go wrong!

2. Joy secures our heritage

Joy is an evidence of our trust in God, that He can perform all that he had promised us. It goes further to secure all our good things, not only does our bones dry up while we are bitter; it dries up our ban, which we could call our source of livelihood. Joel 1:12 keeps our eyes on this truth "**The vine is dried up, and the fig tree languisheth; the pomegranate tree, the palm tree also, and the apple tree, even all the trees of the field, are withered: because joy is withered away from the sons of men.** When joy is lacking in us, many good things will also lack in us, that is why Christ encourages us to stay joyful at all times; He understands the secret of remaining ever joyful. Hebrews 12:2 makes that clear "**Looking unto Jesus the author and finisher of our faith; who for the joy that was set before him endured the cross, despising the shame, and is set down at the right hand of the throne of God.** If we can neglect the high tides staring us in the face, while we seek genuine joy; days will come you can't remember some issues were before you, for how they will be sorted out would definitely be a surprise to you. Every secret supplement the body requires to stay healthy is stored in JOY!

Prayer: The only sadness, darkness that would ever remain in you, is that which the authority of Christ Jesus can't subdue; because there is no such authority ever existing anywhere in the world; begin now to walk in freedom in the name of Jesus Christ. Amen! Psalms 62:11 says "**God hath spoken once; twice have I heard this; that power belongeth unto God**. Every manipulation of satan that can't stand the authority of God will never have effect over your life anymore in the name of Jesus Christ. Amen!

Beloved, this article is for the edification of the body of Christ, that we all as Christians will always stay in faith; believing that God who loved us so much, gave us his only begotten son, not just for us to be saved alone, but help others know this truth. The knowledge of this truth puts every one of us back in the place of dominion. You can share this article as a gift of love to another soul, let's do our part raising giants for Christ. I love you, all the way from Africa; Nigeria precisely! If you would like to send a prayer request, or have any personal information you would like to share with me; kindly write an email to me. Shephardshouse90@gmail.com.

Your testimony is welcome!

Look out for my other book "REDEMPTION" for you faith building